LOVE, PLEASURE, AND PAIN
THE ANATOMY OF ADULTERY

```
POET, MADMAN, MYSTIC
AUTOBIOGRAPHY OF A POET IN POETRY

BOOK II
THE PHOENIX TRILOGY
```

Daylight Publishing **Roy. E. Day Jr.**
With Lulu Publishing

Edited and Cover by Helen Manget

Dedication

To my parents, especially thank to my father for his financial support of this project, siblings and their children, my friends, cousins, spiritual teachers and to this beautiful planet, our Mother Earth.

Introduction

This three book autobiography in poetry covers the first forty years of my life, with the poetry starting at seventeen. I have attempted to make it primarily poetry, but have supplied enough prose to provide context for the interested. It was collected and first edited in 1994 and although published   years later the original time frame,   attitude, and perspective was retained.

Table of Contents

Meeting and Beginning End of Winter `83 6
    I Died Daily 7
    Open Invitation 9
    You Ask Me Why I Don't Look For Love 10
    You Use the Phrase "Young Man" Too Much 11
    It's Way Too Late To Turn Back Now 14
    As I Would Expect Any Man 15
    Psychologist Seduces Mystic 16
    My Body Shudders at the Thought of You So Close 18
    A Vision of the Goddess - Love in the South 18
    Balance 20

Love Strengthens - Separation by Distance Spring `84 22
    The Essence of Our Feeling 23
    I Don't Like Being Repetitious 24
    A Relative Falls Gravely Ill - You Aid the Healing Ritual 24
    Whispered in the Wind 26
    Up the Stakes 27
    I Missed You 27
    You Couldn't Freely Talk 29
    Discovering 30
    Shaman Waiting 31
    Leaving for Fieldwork - the Call of my Career 31
    Cutting Edge 32
    Forty-eight Hours 33
    Tomcat Calling 34
    The Worst Drug 35
    West Texas 36
    Often It's the Dark 37
    Knowing That You Love Me 38
    Words Fail 39
    I've Known Women With the Strength of Will Before 40
    Reuniting With Laura 40
    Don't Even Say 41
    Living at the Base of Mount Whitney 42
    Spring In Berkeley, 1984 43
    Not Enough 43

  Not A Tear 44
  Night Flight Over San Francisco 45
  Eight Long Weeks 45

The Summer of Our Love Coming Home - Shipwrecked At the Folk Summer '84 47
  Fanned the Flames 48
  Shadows of the Moon 49
  Dreams 49
  This Body Thing 50
  On the Side 52
  Tunnel's End 53
  When We Met 54
  Solar Winds Howl Throughout My Mind 55
  Waiting by the Phone 56
  Your Husband on the Phone 57
  Failed the Morals Test 59
  Thunderstorms 60
  What I thought Would Happen 63
  After A Pipe 64
  Reform 65
  With Whom You Sleep 66
  As Well As You 68
  Sick 70
  Day by Day 71
  My Red Haired Friend Has Stepped Into A World Of Secrets 72
  Jealous 73

The Waxing of the Summer Moon Summer '84 74
  Love Comes Over Me Like A Wave 75
  Dreams Bear Fruit 76
  Still Desperate 77
  Aphrodite 78
  Love Burns Hot 79
  Honey on the Spoon 80
  Eternal Spring 81
  Not Self Torture - but Salvation 82
  Trump Card 83
  On Demand 84
  Love Burns Hotter 85
  Do Anything 86
  Hot Winds of August 87

- Keep Falling 88
- Songs on the Radio 89
- Perfectly Matched 90
- Sharks in the Swimming Pool 92
- The Stupidity of It 92
- The Angel Standard Time Zone 94
- The Dinner Party and Your Best Friend 95
- More Rare Than Precious 97
- Keep on Smiling Through 99
- Second Fight 99
- Casting Stones 100
- My Daemon Waiting 101
- Sweet Reassurance 102
- Inconsistency and Discernment 103
- Screaming in my Mind 104
- A Modern Woman 107
- When Not With Me 107
- Pain-Rimmed Eyes 108
- Impasse 109
- Prettiest Face 111
- More Love 112
- The Time for Our Love is Now 113

Waning of the Summer Moon 115
- Lifetime Record 116
- Seek the Mystery of the Goddess 117
- Undercurrents 117
- Tired But Lovely 120
- Moon Kiss 122
- Not Laughing 123
- The Weeping Whiners of Your Life 124
- Gentle Rest 126
- Missing You 127
- Pull-Back Time 129
- If You Were Available 130

The Fall Means Winter Comes Autumn `84 138
- Cold Hard Words on the Phone 139
- Expecting You to Call 140
- Don't Tempt the Barely Saved 142
- Tactless 145

- Method of Your Madness 151
- Every Time 154
- Not Your Buddy 155
- Gabrielle Draws Beside Me 157
- Handcuffs 158
- Gabrielle 159
- I Refuse 161
- Not Alone 162
- Worse Than Me 166
- Having Peace 169
- Husband Calling 170
- Your Husband Asks Me to Stay Away 171
- Supposed To Do 173
- All Love's Must End 174
- The Bitter Risk of Sweet Adultery 175
- Mimosa Blooms in the Summertime 176

After the Fall Winter `84, and 1985 179
- Deportee 181
- Spring Rain 183
- Like We Were Sixteen 184
- June Night 185
- Violent Passages 186
- Chance Encounter 188
- You Looked So Different 189

Meeting and Beginning End of Winter `83

Preamble - Confessions of a Fallen Mystic

I Died Daily

Hurt, Hate, and Anger took me from the Light into the Darkness

Something about the lure of Death made me stay

For two years I died daily in the bottle

For two years I was a slave unto cocaine

And when finally, like a dog

I scent-marked the lowest gutter

with the utter wretch of Unlife

I crawled so slowly upwards

from the grave that I'd been digging

and I chose Life again.

While the first book of this trilogy concerns my spiritual search, this second book is primarily an expression of romantic poetry. This book traces a relationship from start to finish. From this and later experiences I've learned that most adulterous relationships have much in common. Hopefully this book will highlight some of the patterns and pitfalls of such relationships. I am in no way approving or condoning adultery. But it certainly happens, always has, always will.

This book begins with the end of the winter of '83 and the spring of '84 at a time I had returned to college and was pursuing an education in symbolic anthropology. Although I had come a long way from the patterns of alcohol and cocaine abuse that I had fallen into during and after the failures of my business and relationship in Athens, I was not totally abstaining, and had some lapses. But in general, this was a positive time of learning.

When I met May she was a psychology professor at a college outside Atlanta and I was a student at Georgia State. Before I met May my brother had told me that I would find May attractive and intelligent, but that she was married and unavailable. She was from a wealthy old-Atlanta family, whose name I immediately recognized.

Open Invitation

I know the mores of our culture

and the ring upon your finger

agree that I should remain mute

But I like you, find you interesting

and wish to be your friend.

That's open-ended, but not pressing

seems to me we do attract

Your eyes are steady when I look at you

I can feel you looking back

Your eyes are really beautiful

and you carry yourself well

You know that I've been watching you

and you've checked me out as well

So if you'd like to keep a secret

or simply have another friend

        come visit me for lunch one day

        or come by some afternoon.

You Ask Me Why I Don't Look For Love

I've carried you in my thoughts

    and you're here now

I enjoyed our evening

    but you sound incredulous

when I tell You that I don't look for love

and you almost seem to pressure me

    to go looking for that love.

Try to understand

    I've got too much to accomplish

somebody who might want to fill my time

    would be too weighty a distraction

I've adapted in a way that suits my needs

so far unencumbered by emotions.

But you've come in and rocked the boat.

You ask me why I'm not looking for somebody

You tell me its what everybody needs

Well I've had it all before, and I always found the door

because that's me, that's what I need.

Women like you are the reason I'm not looking.

You Use the Phrase "Young Man" Too Much

You use the phrase "young man" too much

you haven't done the bleeding

you haven't lain in a broken pile

with those whom Death has gathered

You haven't watched your own blood pour out

it's pungent, bright, and sticky

you haven't had your face sewn up

or spent months in one position

You may have looked at a gun before

if so, that's to your credit

when your life is the squeeze of a stranger's hand

it changes shades of meaning

To live with danger, pain, and death

affects deep levels of one's being

for ears to hear and eyes to see

there is wisdom for the gleaning.

You call me young, I have to laugh

I can't believe you mean it

all those years you spent in school

I spent in hard core living.
By the time I became a legal adult

just two years after you did

I had used up two of my cat's nine lives

and compiled two felony convictions.

For years I've tended to shun emotions

you say that I sound bitter

but bitter or wary, the damage done

was enough to give me reason

I know I've learned from risk and pain

but it wasn't academic

I cannot view myself as young

or think of you as older.

It's Way Too Late To Turn Back Now

It's way too late to turn back now

I really wouldn't want to

You say that we'll be friends for life and accidental lovers

all that sounds just well and fine

to be with you is joyous

but it makes me deny my strong desire

for those things you can't offer.

But even when we are alone

I feel eyes above my shoulder

I want to be with you alone

with some psychic isolation

and simply let this love come out

you know my dam is breaking

You used the word "love" to my surprise

Its time has come for making.

As I Would Expect Any Man

Maybe I'm the little brother You never made love to

      Maybe it's that you've <u>only</u> been married four years

I don't know.

      I don't want to know the reasons for your actions

or why You want to make love with me

      I do not know.

I held back with much reserve and let you lead

      I held back at least as well

as I would expect any man to do with my wife

      if I had one.

Psychologist Seduces Mystic

As I move about my daily world

I see glimpses from last night

Your beauty as I held You

our love, finally, let out

And I want You at this moment

our next session to begin

as we learn about each other's love

to make and take and give again

It will only grow much warmer

when we share our fire again

I won't indulge my mystic nature

but never laugh like that again

the word shaman shares the same root word

with the word for ecstasy

I had given you that feeling

yet you laughed at my beliefs

I will never give you half a chance

to laugh at me again

If what I believe is so damn funny

you'll have to do with one less man.

Your Love Within My Aura

I did not bathe this evening

as I'd planned before retiring

I left the smell of You upon me

the scent of love within my aura

And whenever I close my eyelids

my inner eye sees blond hair shining

I see your eyes, your smile, your lovely face

and I am awestruck by Love's beauty.

My Body Shudders at the Thought of You So Close

I lie thinking, playing pictures in my mind

      and remembering Sunday night

there was tenderness and pleasure

      frustration and fulfillment

and my body shudders at the thought of You so close

      a physical reaction to the mental image of our love-making

the way You give love, the way You take love

      don't let anything I've ever said about your strength

dissuade You from the certainty

      of your overwhelming femininity.

A Vision of the Goddess - Love in the South

I don't know when I ceased to fight your love

      but when I finally dropped my guard

I know it swept me like a flood

      and now I fight to regain control

a control I thought I'd always hold

    until You.

You come into my life

    like a vision of the Goddess

I steal into your heart

    like a thief in the night

in the misty vapor round the Moon

    our love is blessed in golden light

and in a way more mystical than physical

    our love has seemed to come alive

as a force of passion and healing

    a source of joy in both our lives.

The soil is rich and red and brown here

    and is fertile to my soul

the oak trees stand tall, proud, and majestic

    their roots reach deep into the soil

and I want You like the oak tree

    needs the rain to live and grow

and I want You with a feeling

    that I'd forgot, or never known.

Balance

Like the Oak tree in the winter wind

    the branches twisting under pressure

still in the cold and darkness I survived

    my questions echoed in the silence

Your love is healing to my soul

    brings healing to my life

Once more I rise up from the Darkness

    to find balance in the Light.

Although I feel these poems are fairly self-explanatory, and revealing enough to let the reader know what's going on, sometimes a few explanations are necessary.

May's husband was a local musician, who spent most of his time in the night life or in entertainment environments. He had cheated on May and confessed. That was right before we met.

May and I started going out. She and her husband talked about trying an open marriage, not exactly a common thing in Georgia. They decided to continue as normal, with their usual routines and sexual relations. But in their free time, they were free. I told May that there were two old girlfriends I saw occasionally, and she said that was fine, and only fair considering.

Love Strengthens - Separation by Distance Spring `84

The Essence of Our Feeling

The Essence of the peace of Midnight

or the gentle touch of the Spring breeze

is love.

The Essence of the silver crescent

and the splendor of the golden orb

is love.

The Essence of my spirit

which I see and feel as Light

is love.

And the Essence of the feeling

that we both know we share between us

that Flows back and forth between us

touching spirits, minds, and bodies

emotions almost overwhelming

the true Essence of Our feeling

is Love.

I Don't Like Being Repetitious

I don't like being repetitious

But I'm feeling quite incredulous

That things have gone so well

so fast

so far

Without doing any harm,

and so we continue

to experience

this growing love

and our inner healing.

A Relative Falls Gravely Ill - You Aid the Healing Ritual

I can't help but want more of You

or feel our time is not enough

So my week is spent in thinking about

or seeing You in my mind

I long to feel your body

when I lie alone at night

But what You give to me is much more

than just the pleasures of the Night

You've brought so many good things

that I really can't explain

but tonight You brought me peace of mind

during deep sorrow and dark pain

But there is a transcendental beauty

to Life's necessity for pain

I was thankful for your helping

as we worked in an ancient, Indian way

Tonight You healed me, soothed me, helped me

with the love You freely gave

so my emotions overflow now

and I thank Life for You again.

Whispered in the Wind

I heard the Name of God whispered in the Wind

it was Light upon my soul

I heard the Voice of Mother Earth in the bubbling brook

bespeaking Her love for All

Whom upon Her body dwell

And I feel as a Reality

the touching of our souls

Is all Life not Both

physical and Mystical

rational and non-material

and all the other

resolved dualities

which come together

to comprise the Whole.

Up the Stakes

        Your name is one husband behind

        and it feels your heart is two

        I've got these strong love feelings

        But it seems the hurt is growing too

        If You knew how bad I want You

        You would understand the pain

        But you're so damn busy, Miss Professor

        You don't want to up the stakes.

I Missed You

I told my brother that I missed You

    the short time you've been away

But I'll hear from You tomorrow

    and in three nights we can play

I can't wait to hear about it

    I deeply need to hold you tight

This week could have gone much smoother

    if I'd talked to You each night

I missed the shared ideas and feelings

    missed your astute career advice

it hasn't hit me that I'm leaving

    that I'll be gone for all that time

I'm sure your husband's very happy

    to have you all, all to himself

But I knew we'd have to talk sometime

    You tell me when to call collect

and we can always touch in spirit

    we had an instant psychic link

from that first time that we made love

    did we not feel our two souls meet

and our love holds such strong promise

    that we can be healed, whole, and complete.

You Couldn't Freely Talk

Though I knew You couldn't freely talk

    it still felt really good

just to hear your voice again

    and hear what's happening in your world

its only been a few short days

    but it seems a longer time

I guess that's cause you're far away

    yet a constant on my mind

So here I am a freedom-freak

and there You are with your wedding ring

and here we stay in a love so new

        so strong

           and growing

    And now I leave.

Discovering

We made sweet love this evening

What I'd wanted all week long

I'd spent six days and nights without You

and the seventh day alone

Yeah, we made sweet love this evening

and we talked, and smiled, and hugged

As we discover who each other is

what we think and what we've done

As we watch this love grow deeper

it seems stronger every day

we have passion's fire, and gentle times

and share the hope that love will stay

Shaman Waiting

There's a Paiute Shaman in the desert

    and other healers out there too

and a Sweatlodge I belong to

    and I'm four years overdue

It's the next step in my new career

    and the next step for my soul

this is what I have to do now

    You know I wish You'd come along.

Leaving for Fieldwork - the Call of my Career

To leave the South in blooming Springtime

    after finding brand new love

Is just about the dumbest thing

    that I think I've ever done.

To leave love is a carnal sin

    and the true act of a fool

but its the right thing for my new career

    I pray it doesn't cost me You.

Cutting Edge

You say I'm pushy and that's funny

    cause I'm feeling pushed aside

You're so angry at my leaving

    ground your cutting edge so fine

It's a good time for my leaving

    or so You said to me

Its exciting, but I'll miss your touch

    and I'll miss your smiling face.

Forty-eight Hours

So much has happened in my career this week

You weren't available to talk

and the thought I'm gone for weeks or months soon

is not much help at all

But we share so few hours

if we're lucky, twice a week

if I'm gone as long as two months

we'll miss forty-eight hours under the sheets

But this build me up - to pull me down

this playing second base

is not as easy as its been before

at times, it drives me near insane.

Tomcat Calling

I hear the tomcat growling outside

I could swear he calls my name

But I know its just the cat in me

I know that we're the same

And as my mind turns now to you

in some way we're opposites

Yet You prove to me you're naughty

while my life is filled with risk

And while my mind does dwell on You

I see we're different, but the same

now You can't believe I'm leaving

and I can't believe you'll stay.

The Worst Drug

Well now I've got a reason

to quit this dangerous situation

Off an On for fifteen years

    I lived the lifestyle of an outlaw

and though I've never robbed nobody

    never had to shoot no-one

I've seen lot's of real good people get sent-up

    and lots more go down the tubes

I ain't the one to do no preaching

    I seen the pot, I seen the coke

but I ain't never hurt nobody

    Just seen some lives get wrecked past hope

I've seen it come and watched it go

    the pot

        the coke

            the drugs

                the booze

    and in my mind there is no doubt

        that of them all

                booze is the worst

I've seen the drink take weak and strong

                alcohol's the worst of all.

West Texas

Of course, I saw You there tonight

    in the fullness of the Moon

the empty spaces of west Texas

    found my mind was filled with You

Its only been three months, still,

    You react so much like me

you'll be getting all your work caught up

    trying not to think of me

yet I'll be there in the nighttime

You'll see my face before you sleep

and You'll see me in the golden Moon

    although I'd swear she wears your face

I feel our love here in my body

    it fills my mind, my heart, my soul

its become an ever present feeling

    has helped to heal, and make me whole.

Often It's the Dark

It's not always the bright side of Life

    that brings knowledge

Often, it's the Dark

It's difficult to measure love

    In happiness brought by your lover's presence

Easier to judge by depth of longing

      desperation of need

                           extent of anguish

when deprived

of your lover's presence.

Knowing That You Love Me

                Just loving You, and talking to You

                and knowing that You love me too

                Keeps me going and pulls me through

                despite your long pauses and threats on the phone

                despite all my anger and pushing for more.

Words Fail

As I try to write how beautiful and feminine You are

my words fail

like pebbles thrown against a castle wall

like water cascading over the cliffs of Yosemite

failing to was those rocks away

my words fail

but give to me the chance

the time, the years

and let my actions and my touch

and not my words express the thought

and You will know my meaning.

I've Known Women With the Strength of Will Before

I've known women with the strength of will before

I've known women of acute awareness

I've loved one once that was in your league

but after three years I left her

But by your side I feel at home

and she's ten years your junior

You and I are of the same generation

at times our souls reflect like mirrors.

Reuniting With Laura

I cleared the air here

      and I feel much better

it's always better just to tell the truth

      it's harder, but it's simpler.

It's hard to fake it, anyway

      when my heart's a thousand miles away

but she's a good and loving friend

      and she accepts my ways.

Don't Even Say

I don't want to hear this self-indulgent bullshit

      that it's harder on You for me to call

that it makes You miss me more

      I don't want to hear that kind of trash

I need to talk to You

      I have to talk to You

to share

      to get your thoughts and ideas

I need your mind

      I want your body

I know that we've touched souls

      touched souls

Don't even say things

    like "if we're still together this summer"

You know we will be

    don't tell me to come home

with that compelling tone in your voice

    for six hours in a hotel room

Promise me time, promise me time

    because I'm coming home, my love

        I'm coming home.

Living at the Base of Mount Whitney

I sit here eating, taking in Mount Whitney's glory

at a big window in the kitchen

as a clear cold mountain stream bubbles on by

I am surrounded by God's Beauty

and still, my mind is filled with You

and You keep telling me, on the phone, to come home

but whose home, I ask and wonder

whose home?

Spring In Berkeley, 1984

I lent the black hooker next door a dollar in change

She showed me her two fifty dollar bills

said she'd made it in ten minutes

but didn't want to break them

I shared my pizza with her, too

she really was quite friendly

I asked her what the streets were like these days

and found her more scared of AIDS than anything.

Not Enough

Talking to You on the phone is not enough

I just want to come on home

to see the South in the Springtime

to be with You and share our love.

I want to be with You in the morning

      commune in mind throughout the day

I want to love You in the nighttime

    flat out fuck the world away.

It's weeks, if not a month

before I hold You in my arms

but I'd have been there yesterday

were You free in heart and mind.

Not A Tear

    The black hooker next door likes me

    said she'd try to find me a joint

    she was waiting on white powder

    I lent her change to buy a coke

    that's twice this trip it's happened

    the lady next door was up for sale

    and they both told me quite sad stories

    but neither shed a tear.

Night Flight Over San Francisco

It's a night flight over San Francisco

the lights look pretty way down there

I know I'll miss the desert

and my chance for healing there

But I've missed You now for so long

I've counted more than seven weeks

I don't want to live without You

yet You can't even meet halfway

Don't You know I really love You

Don't You know I'll wreck your life

It's so bad how much I need You

that I can't tell wrong from right.

Eight Long Weeks

After eight long weeks I held You

and You were silken in my arms

those lonely weeks and half-veiled threats

    added accent to your charm

Tonight we finally made sweet love

    smooth silk transformed in passion's fire

one touch and smile was all I needed

    to let all questions fall aside.

The Summer of Our Love Coming Home - Shipwrecked At the Folk Summer '84

Fanned the Flames

I revel in the joy and beauty Life has brought to me

I symbolically thank the golden Moon for our sweet love

I have been reborn and am becoming whole again

I am re-joining with and re-discovering who I am.

You have kindled flames of love in me

You sparked the fire, You fanned the blaze

My passion grows and yearns for You

these deep desires of lust that you enflame

Now I'm aiming all the strength of my love at You

and I'm trusting in the golden myth of love

that love truly is a beneficent force in Nature

that can satiate the hungers of the soul.

Shadows of the Moon

I love the hours after midnight

and shadows cast by the Moon

I love to watch fog billowing off the water at night

and making love to You

I love the feel of the west wind

flowing warm across my face

and I love being inside You - connected

Love flowing back and forth in waves.

Dreams

I've had a couple of good shots at love before

but I intentionally blew them

there's an outside chance I'll live my dreams

these days You seem to fill them.

This Body Thing

I wrestle with my inner thoughts

    I know my inner feelings

But as You succinctly said

    this is risky business

I know that Life is not a game

    still, I'm playing this thing honest

I tried doing what felt right

    I tried talking to your husband

He sent the message through you that it was okay

    But he didn't want to meet me

So now I freely give my love to You

    Be warned, it carries danger

and though its only of emotions

    they affect one's freedom.

Now compulsion drives me to the phone

    Those times I can't see You

these word confused   -   as is my mind

    unbridled feelings flowing

I feel them in You

    can see them, touch them

You never would have risked this much

    Without the reality of shared feelings

You risk too much

    but it seems so slowly

I push and pull

    am always wanting

but this body thing, alone

        has me hooked

            and intrigued.

On the Side

I'm sitting here working

and I'm glad You finally called

You asked me out for this weekend

tonight You celebrate at home

So for four years now you're married

and today You shed your tears

at the happiness and the memories

of the years you've shared with him

and I'm happy that you're happy

it seems things have worked out fine

You've got your marriage and profession

and a lover on the side.

Tunnel's End

This time last year I hadn't met You yet

    I'd been back in school one quarter

after eight long years of laying out

    and living like an outlaw

I tried to se if I could beat it

    beat the coke and booze alone

or if I'd have to seek real help

    from people who preface their name like You

Now, I think that even then, I knew about the coming Light

    that waited at that tunnel's end

But I couldn't see or feel that Light

    until I held You in my arms

I could not make that Light my own

    until I won your heart

You were so sweet that first night

    we were both so nervous

but there was magic in our loving

    and in our coming together.

When We Met

The Darkness was slowly giving way

    I'd already made great strides

I was taken when I met You

    so quickly

You touched something deep inside.

I always took You very seriously

I didn't want to make any mistakes

I knew You were worth the effort

I knew I'd do what it takes.

Solar Winds Howl Throughout My Mind

Solar winds howl throughout my mind

    my heart is filled with You

the Moon eclipses the Sun today

    altogether too much like You

My best friend has seen my loves come and go

    he's never known me to share a lover

he's so amazed at my compromising

    his advice he keeps withholding

and I long for wisdom whispered somewhere

    yet no solutions come

there is no one

      no place, no other heart

but ours, to bear this load

but what is cost and what is hurt

      this weight upon the soul

how does one gauge the strength of love

      or the value of true joy.

Waiting by the Phone

Sitting by the phone, waiting for You

      sometimes I think that's all I do

in my mind and in my heart

      a raging storm, a blazing fire

I would give anything I can think of

to whatever God or Goddess there may be

to have You lay beside me every night

to love You endlessly.

Your Husband on the Phone

I'm lying here

rubbing vitamin E all over my body

hoping for quick healing

and thinking about You

I've had one month

to integrate my personality

old and new

spiritual and sensual

disciplined and indulgent

and I find I have to lay down my own rules

make self-commitments

to guide me through the maze

of rationalities

of rights and wrongs

to guide me through to find

a morality of Nature.

I talked to your husband on the phone

he was looking for You

calling at my parent's house

I was less than thrilled

I said I'd talked to You recently

that You had something to do

exactly what, I did not know

so I told him the truth

he sounded polite

almost gentle or kind

he was looking for his wife

I was less than happy

but I know he's got the right

still, I find it disquieting

that he called me up at all

it makes the fact that you're married

seem more real than it did before.

Failed the Morals Test

Maybe I failed the morals test
when I turned down
the way out that You offered
but maybe I passed
because I listened to my heart
We're both confused
and there's not much chance or hope
that this situation
will bring either of us
the needed rest or a quiet heart

but God knows I want You

in so many ways

I might even need You

at least it feels that way

and I do treasure what we have

and I don't take it lightly

but I would take more than You give

but for now, there is the moment

we have so much Life and Love today

in a world so full of problems

I feel a joy words cannot say

and my heart remains excited.

Thunderstorms

My little sister asked me how I am

    I said depressed and angry, lonely, sad

so she asked me how You were and I said fine

    that I was just angry at the situation

But it's more than that, and more than what we said today

      it's more what she said yesterday

that I wouldn't want someone who was available.

I don't know what I'm doing, or why

      am I trying to cut the balls off some nameless man

who stole my woman years ago

      by doing the same thing

to some other nameless man, over and over

      I don't know, I just don't know anymore

I can tell that you're confused

      you're as inconsistent as a changing wind

as unpredictable as a thunderstorm in May

      but I need your love, I want your love

it's the only thing I want, for now

      but what about tomorrow?

You said your fantasy was your husband and me

      and I got weekends

well what about the lonely week, You want too much

    and me, hypocrite that I am

with plans and maps and globe in hand

    and an ego big enough to try

and You strong willed, committed

    do You really feel love for your husband

or just repeat it

    You got what You were looking for

I got exactly what I asked for

    and we both feel love

we say it, we know it

    and with great pleasure our bodies show it

barely, barely just beginning to express that love

    I need You so much.

But need is wrong, I want you, I want You so much

    but I'll survive no matter what, and so will You

for I've survived so much, so much already

    I've seen the broken

in hospitals and nursing homes

      their spirits more than bodies broken

but I've survived, survived

      and You yourself can feel my healing

You who are a catalyst for that psychological healing

      and the special reason for its succeeding.

What I thought Would Happen

I don't know what I thought would happen

      when I returned home

But I was living in my dreams

Reality may be better

      at least in the long run, so it seems

for reality holds the promise of a future

      while our love stays strong today

still, I want You badly all the time

you're on my mind both night and day

I'll find more balance as time passes

    or learn how to function this obsessed

your fantasies are not so bad

    still, mine suit my taste best.

After A Pipe

I feel saliva in my beard

    from smoking long and hard my Sacred Pipe in healing ritual

the sensation brings me no discomfort or unease

    the wetness reminds me of our passion

the sweet taste of You upon my tongue

    is a sensation I desire

and the ecstasy You bring to me

    more than fulfills my strong desires.

I want to hold You in the morning

when I'm rising from my sleep

I want to hold You in the evening

when I feel, so strong, the need

I long to love You after midnight

at those times I'm most alive

I want to ravish you and adore You

in the Moon's soft magic light.

Reform

                    She thinks that I'm withdrawing my love

                    when I only draw within

                    decisions made cause me inner strife

                    and she can't understand

I want, so much, to make her proud

I want to share strong love

she pulls away when I won't conform

and I label her reformist

I confess my sins and explain their causes

she hears but won't respond

I need to hold her in my arms again

and renew this special love.

With Whom You Sleep

Tonight I know with whom You sleep

and I've been with someone else

tears well up within my eyes

but I refuse to weep

This whole thing should bring happiness

you've brought great joy to me

I guess we both must balance

what we want with what must be

When we questioned Fate, the future

in the symbols of Tarot

I saw your power visible

that You are powerful we both know

but let me live my own life

take the chances that I choose

I won't complain about your husband

hell, who could tell You what to do?

You're a very strong willed woman

and I'm a strong willed man

and the love we have seems lasting

just beginning to expand

I'd like to work together sometime

it seems we'll always be good friends

and Our summer's only starting

there's so much Life here to be lived

I don't want to waste a second

cause we've both got tons to do

but I want to grow much closer

I want to know the secret You.

As Well As You

It's obvious I can't go from person to person

as well as You

I'm out of practice

especially at this "day to day"

and I can't always see the world your way

but no two people ever see the same

You began a romance with what You called a risk

well I'm a lesser risk today

My established goals are still the same

I'm a much better risk today.

The season is summer, the feeling is love

and the opportunity is the moment

can't you see that I've sacrificed for my freedom

the risks I take are not because I'm bored

but because I can't be wasting time

shipwrecked at my parents house.

The love we found before springtime

is the excitement of my life

don't let love go cause we disagree

I need You in my life.

Sick

I joke and say it's sick of us

when I say sick, I mean holds pain

something here seems strange enough

but this love I don't disdain.

This summer holds much hope and joy

the promise of work completed

I'm seeing progress on so many fronts

and our love keeps growing deeper.

Day by Day

You've got your husband and a home life

      and me at beck and call

so it's crazy i feel guilty

      giving someone else my love.

Maybe it's transition

      I can't do it day by day

to give my love to first one heart

      and then another that same day.

You know I want You to myself

      that I'd give to You my all

don't pull away from love this rare

      don't let this white-hot flame grow cold.

My Red Haired Friend Has Stepped Into A World Of Secrets

My red haired friend has stepped into a world of secrets

    I helped take her there

Although she's free-er now, and more herself

    she will play the liar's game

I want to love You all my lifetime

    and now You say you've had to lie

to a man You love and will not leave

    and this strange world turns on by

And I'm to find my path and way

    using tools of Dark and Light

I know I'm meaning well to all

    but the law I stay outside

You feel rejected, but won't for long

    it's my chaos, not our decline

It's true my mind was distracted

    but that happened only twice.

Jealous

You say I don't miss a chance

    to make You jealous

it's not conscious

    but I know it's true

But I'm always jealous of your husband

    what am I supposed to do?

I won't continue to make You jealous

    now I know that I succeed

what starts as playful, soon turns hurtful

    and in excess of the need.

The Waxing of the Summer Moon Summer '84

Love Comes Over Me Like A Wave

Ray Charles keeps singing "I can't stop loving you"

and love comes over me like a wave

If You could feel what You do, inside me

You would have to be amazed.

I know this feeling can't last forever

at least not this intense

And Life is always changing

or so its been explained

But at least we have these moments

the best hours of each week

We share a rare and mutual love

that much we plainly see.

I feel sorry for your husband

even though he must hate me

You're so honest with your feelings

does it really set You free?

Dreams Bear Fruit

We wrote a poem together

    lying in a hotel room

it's all about sadness and frustration

    and wanting a place to love

So now I re-read the poem we wrote together

    at the hotel where we'd love

Now I'm lying on the bed we share

    at the apartment that You found.

I love this place, it suits me well

    I was stifled where I was

and You're trying hard to spend time here

    I haven't felt too much alone.

I know that Life's not a fantasy

    Yet here's a dream we made come true

There are other dreams that we both share

    that may likewise bear sweet fruit.

Still Desperate

    I told my brother about my new apartment

    You know he sounded pleased

    He guessed I wouldn't be so desperate to see You

    now that we have a place

    I disagreed, I don't know why

    but I'm still desperate for your love

    Is it the threat of losing You?

    or is this just too good?

But the future holds some rocky roads

separation at some time

I'll have to go to graduate school

You need a better job

But for now, I call this Eden

and now, this is our time

You try to keep your husband

I'll try for peace for mind.

Aphrodite

I prayed to the Moon and the Goddess of Love

the Goddess sent me You.

Thirteen Moons make a year complete

Thirteen roses brought by You

Thirteen candles burn to thank the Moon

and bless this exquisite love

Thirteen times may our love grow stronger

Stronger and deeper than at first.

Love Burns Hot

I think about our time last night

You healed me once again

whether intuition or instinct

You always understand

You give to me the kind of love

that fills the moment's needs

last night, and the night before

were new highs of ecstasy.

Honey on the Spoon

I've seen love flow sweet before

    like honey from the spoon

        before

            but last night

                love flowed sweeter

I've felt love burn hot before

    and flow like molten lava

        before

            but last night

                love flowed hotter

And now I'm looking forward

    to the day and to the night

        when my life is healed

           and your life is free

              and love flows between us

                  unceasingly.

Eternal Spring

        The mimosa flowers bright pink in Georgia

          in the southern Summer sun

          in August, though, they lighten color

          and in the fall drop to the ground

        for nine months now, our tree still flowers

        for nine months now, our tree still blooms

      and at this moment, we know what love means

      at this moment we live the "eternal Spring".

Not Self Torture - but Salvation

I sit here late at night

    torturing myself

running through my insecurities

    of how, in some ways,

I cannot compare, cannot compete

And now, I smile, and watch within my mind

    that time when I had called the Goddess out

Done the invocation

    and as I started to pull away

You said "oh no! oh no! Don't go away"

    You made my day that night

You made my week.

Trump Card

I wish I had some trump card to play

      some gentle, harmless magic spell

to fully steal your love away

the truth that we've both found

      is that hurt comes with love

and there are few harmless ways

But I have the peace of the spirit

      it's infectious

and I know you want it too

      inner peace of the spirit

You don't get that there at home

      or from his love, do You?

On Demand

Last night You made my week worthwhile

my friends can't understand

they think that I act foolish

because You wear a wedding band

But they don't know, cause they're not there

when we let our love pour down

My God, You are so beautiful

every time, it still astounds

You told me what I wanted to hear

You made my ego proud

because everyone should be the best

at something in this world

If, as You say, I am the best

the best you've ever had

my talents, I do offer now

for a lifetime, on demand.

Love Burns Hotter

I woke up smiling in the morning

    we had laid in love all night

You said you'd never felt it flow so strong

    as pure love poured out our hearts

Last night was fun and joyous

    filled with pleasure through and through

I don't want to lose this feeling

    and I won't let go of You

I know this love is unique

    its inspiration seems divine

You show and say You love me just as much

    so I'll hold on through time.

I told her she made love like I used to

naturally   -   as a child

I was so silent   -   so serious

until I broke

and let some small sound out.

Do Anything

Remember when You said to me

You'd wear sexy lingerie, do anything

Anything to please me

and You were amazed at yourself that way.

I marvel at myself and think

in a way so similar, it seems to me

that I would do anything   -   whatever it takes

Anything to make You happy - Any thing, Any way.

Hot Winds of August

The hot winds of August are blowing through my mind

a mind so set on You

We share a fire that has flamed to new heights

set long ago by You

I've seen and felt and tasted love

and we shared Love last night

with heart-felt passion, I've wooed some women

but last night was unique

I felt our love, I saw our love

glistening in your eyes

this love is real and hot and sweet

like the kind that lasts for life.

Keep Falling

I keep falling deeper in love with You

    although I know the risk

I keep thinking that you're keeping pace

    but You waiver more than me

I know that you're under too much stress

    and it's not easy there at home

        but things with us keep getting better

            so now, I work, and wait for more.

Songs on the Radio

I'm standing in my braces with the radio down low

      they're playing all these love songs

Silly, but they hit home

the one they're playing now says "I'm back on my feet

      and eager to be what You wanted"

You see, I am "lost in love"

      and trying hard to make You happy

and find some peace, too

and now a song says "it's a one in a million

      chance of a lifetime"

with a "one in a million You"

      and I can really relate

I've held the Venuses and the wildcats

      had the wise and loved the wild

but never before a woman who so perfectly

    filled such a beautiful ideal

I worship Nature as a Goddess

    and I worship Nature loving You

but don't be confused, You're the woman I want

    and it's You I make love to.

Perfectly Matched

I tell You that I want You only

I tell You about my other lovers

You say for months, now

there is nothing you'd rather do

than be with me

But - that you'll <u>never</u> leave your husband

That we will <u>never</u> be together

then You make me turn my head

    to see our naked bodies in the mirror

at how perfectly we're matched.

We share a sweet love, a strong love

      a good love

I have since childhood

been seduced by Nature's beauty

that beauty I find so well expressed in You

I adore your modest earlobe

      and your graceful neck and shoulders

I love to press my head against your breasts

      and caress your thin flat stomach

to caress your secret silken hair

      and then worship at your altar

My God, I am in love with You

a love that just grows deeper

Good God, I am in love with You

this love that just gets deeper.

Sharks in the Swimming Pool

You had me worrying about sharks in a swimming pool

losing two day's work, losing two night's sleep

and then You come over like nothing happened

looking happy, and acting sweet.

Two nights ago You were giving warnings

I was making threats, examining options

all because You had a couple of <u>real</u> bad days at home.

Well don't do that to my life, I just don't need it

don't have me going halfway crazy

over nothing, its misleading.

The Stupidity of It

      Sometimes I ponder the stupidity

        of being so in love

with someone so established and committed

basically someone so married

to both her husband and her job

that I get fitted in where time allows

but never for the whole night

never for the weekend

But then we talk and share

and even on the fucking telephone

I feel our love   -   my love   -   your love   -   our love

I can feel our love

and it almost overwhelms me.

Tonight on the phone

I heard truth and reality

I heard the echo of my soul

and I heard your voice

communicate to me your love

and feeling it   -   I am overjoyed and reassured

and in my mind, I am with You.

The Angel Standard Time Zone

I remember, at first, we went Christmas shopping

    and to a play, where we just played

my brother failed to find a present

    You brought a friend - Stephen - to feel safe.

Still you'd call each week and ask me out

    You knew what I desired

I recall with crystal clarity

    when You turned off the lights.

Eight months since then, so much has changed

    infatuation turns to love

we made the dream of a place come true

    yet, last night we drew first blood.

Our anger didn't last too long - we'd rather share the love

I was relieved when You called this morning

    but tonight you seem withdrawn.

So I'll tell You what you've done to me

      and the way I think of time

You've placed me in the Angel Standard Time Zone

      that's where I live my life

time's only meaningful measure

      is in lover's ways and means

I'm always aware of exactly how long

      until we're together once again.

The Dinner Party and Your Best Friend

You brought roses and a vase today

      I called you sweet

I cleaned my house and lit the candles

      You made me wait

Then through the night You look at me with longing eyes

      but with your body, You stay away

As though You might catch some odd disease

      that grows a scarlet letter upon your breast

You looked so ashamed at times.

And yet You, You ask me out, bring me along

      I go and meet your best friend's folks

but I only hear about your own

      and I feel like I'm "the nigga behind the woodpile"

"Is massah Husband gone on yet?"

      But I am not.

I deny this bullshit

      You let other people guilt-trip You

I refuse.

      You and I have done no wrong

We've done no one harm.

So as the night goes on, You seem to show desire

      but act so distant, act so cold

And so when parting comes

      Your friend walks across the room

And gives to me the hug and kiss I needed

      while You turn and walk away without a touch.

Well fuck You cold hearted woman

tomorrow I'll make love

      touch real flesh and bones, feel real passion burn

and think about your coldness on this night.

Are You ashamed of me?

Or are You, as You once warned

      simply void of feelings strong and deep?

Have You become the mother that You despise?

More Rare Than Precious

If it makes You apprehensive

      when I say you're my salvation

then I won't say it.

If I repeat, too much, I love You

      and how You epitomize a feminine ideal

of integrated beauty and intellect

I'll restrain the repetition

      I'll find silence

or new and better ways to say it.

But don't pull your love away.

      Make your work complete and thorough

but don't pull away your love

      Do what You must to save your marriage

if that's what You truly want

      but don't pull your love away.

What we have is more rare than precious

      more special than spiritual

it's healing, it's deepening, it's growing, it's teaching

      and I want to live knowing

that at least in heart, we have and love each other.

Keep on Smiling Through

Three people leave my little place

I become, by contrast, all alone.

The woman I love

so verbally and mentally supportive,

Yet physically   -   so cold

I thought if You said your husband's name again, I'd scream

But instead, I showed You I could smile on through the pain.

I used to smile through dying

Now, I smile and grow in living

and this Summer is and has been

a happy, special time

You won't stay cold.

No, You won't stay so cold.

Second Fight

In the eight months we've been going out

      we almost had our second fight

except You had your curfew

A curfew - much like the night

      I didn't plan

or have much of anything to do with

I went home and got nice clothes

I vacuumed and I washed the car

I shined my shoes   -   got all prepared

and You greeted me at the door   -   with your curfew.

Well that's OK, I understand

your girlfriend's trip, your husbands whims

I understand it.

But still, <u>You</u> changed <u>our</u> plans

I went along and made no sound

it was the only option open.

Casting Stones

So I hear from our friend You're not that mad

well I'd never seen You scream

or throw things around.

There's a small bird on my window sill

the bird's are singing in the sun

I was wrong and I apologize

Let the words be dead and gone

Because it's summer in the Southland

at night the Moon is full and bright

as the fireflies do the dance of light

seeking lovers in the night.

My Daemon Waiting

The waves of Life have crashed me

into a solid rock wall

time and time again

I learned to duck - to bounce - to roll

and I'll survive the wall again

You say I think it's been too good too long

and now I'm <u>looking</u> for the wall

And in my looking I might find - and see - and crash

once more into that wall

That may be true, I hope it's true

that this apprehension is my invention

and my concern begins to wane

and it's probably just my own daemon

waiting at the gate

I've been taught You have to face it all

the deepest Dark inside

and then reunified with the being of Light

cross to the other side

Sweet Reassurance

You knew what needed to be done

      and sweetly did it

I needed reassuring - badly

    You reassured me

I had to see You smile your love at me

    God Knows, I saw it

for two hours we laid   -   not making love

    just lovers touching

I feel like I'm myself again

    with a bright tomorrow

and our love feels like it always has

    overpowering.

Inconsistency and Discernment

I'm waiting on the hopeful verdict

    of a baby yet unborn

and I've thought about some damage done

    I would never cause You harm

Yet my life remains a mystery

      of the beauty and the beast

and now, I try to understand You

      and respect the path You take

Still, You maintain your mystery

      I must discern your subtleties

I must learn to recognize and know

      when it's your heart

           or mind that speaks.

Screaming in my Mind

Surely You heard me screaming in your mind

Felt my shadow nibbling on your earlobe

kissing your fingers   -   and willing them to dial the phone

You must have felt it, I know You felt it

But still, You didn't call

Although I know we didn't plan it

You said your sister's kids would be asleep by seven

I sat by the phone   -   waiting until eight-thirty

waiting   -   waiting to hear how You were, how You felt

waiting   -   waiting to tell You what I'd done

waiting   -

Yet, You did not call

      Why?

Couldn't You feel how concerned about You I was

didn't You feel how badly I wanted to talk

to touch   -   to make contact

I don't understand You

not the full You

Look, I'm waiting in the wings

with all the love within my heart

and I am overwhelmed by my desire to see You well and happy

but don't ignore me

don't categorize me in your life

don't put me on a shelf

or You won't realize

what a kind   -   gentle   -   loving and devoted man

I really am and what a beautiful love we had

until

until by wasting time that could have been ours

and calling your husband after we've just made love

and choosing other's company over mine

You won't realize until -

until I'm gone.

A Modern Woman

You're a thoroughly modern woman

You got your looks   -   your job   -   your breeding

born to a golden family

You can play it so disdainful

You got your man at home   -   housebroken

and all your psychological devices

You've got everything but peace of mind

and multiple orgasms

and You come to me cause You need those things

and others you ain't getting

in your civilized refinement

or with your husband   -   under the blankets.

When Not With Me

It seems you've been unhappy, now, for weeks

    At least when you're not with me

And You say I picked a bad time

    for an outbreak of anger and jealousy

Well I'm sorry you're unhappy

    still, I catch a lot of shit

and you are tough enough to take the flak

    and I'm worth it, every bit

I'll　ease off　-　or I will hit the wall

    but I'll get off your case

but every time You come to me

    You leave smiling

    I bring You hope, and joy, and peace.

Pain-Rimmed Eyes

    I hate to see your pain-rimmed eyes

    But my whole life's been filled with troubled nights

and last night You had a bad one.

I'd rather see your happy smile

and see your eyes so filled with Life

while we share our passion, joy, and fire

now, and forever.

Impasse

Every now and then, every so often

    You reach this point of impasse

when the pressure mounts

    and You search for solutions

and You warn me.

And I can't believe

      that with what we have

either of us, of our own volition

      would choose to live without this love

our love is so much

      so many times throughout the day

our love consumes me.

I feel an unknown fear now   -   to face a life without You

A life without your smiling face

      a life not healed by your embrace

a life I would not want to face

      a life without You.

Life would be so much less rich

      without making love to You.

Sex would be so meaningless

      I would only dream about You.

You are a giver of ecstasy supreme

      and You symbolize the Gracious Goddess

You are an ideal of beauty personified

      and I am so devoted

as a lover, as a friend, and if needed

      in a more ancient way, as a shaman or sorcerer.

We both want, and need, our love.

Prettiest Face

She has the prettiest smile I've ever seen

when she smiles her love up close

I love it when she's here with me

it's what I want the most

I know we've touched in heart and mind

I know that we've touched souls

We both realize what a good thing we have

and I say strongly   -   hold on.

More Love

                I'm no respecter of wedding rings

                I don't deny my childhood's dreams

                      neither do I live them.

                We laid there on the floor last night

            and pure love flowed between our hearts

                a love whose strength is undeniable

The Time for Our Love is Now

I woke up in the foetal position

My first thought was of You

Last night You tried to warn me

and I wonder   -   how could You

just four nights after so much love

You said the most you'd ever felt

And now, You talk of cutting off

You warn, then I make threats.

I came home from California to be with You

I got this apartment with your help

I've changed my life to be with You

hell, You help pay the rent

I've centered so much of my life

around our love

Don't You dare try to cut this off

This *is* the summer of our love.

The time for our love is *now*.

Waning of the Summer Moon

Lifetime Record

You said I was a great and wonderful lover

      which is what every man wants to hear

But I believe You meant it

      there was honesty in your voice.

I wear the perfume of our love

      like the victory wreath of my fondest fantasy

I put off bathing like a little child

      as I wear your love within my aura

I carry your essence on me

      as I carry my love for You within me

and I know contentment.

Seek the Mystery of the Goddess

I seek the goddess when the Moon shines at Night

I seek the Mystery of the Goddess

      in your touch

           and in your eyes

I seek the Mystery of the Goddess in the waters of your love

I seek to touch the Gracious Goddess

both with You and within You

in the Mystery of Love.

Undercurrents

      Friday night was so wonderful and beautiful

      tonight the undercurrents pulled and pushed

          You feel guilty

because your love-light's burning low at home

for the man who wears your ring

while it burns red hot for me.

I don't doubt your love for him

or your passions' fire for me.

Add your guilt to my guilt

for what You know and some things that You don't

plus all the negativity around us

no wonder we had love and war.

Five nights in a row without You

one of which you're only miles away

and I'm willing to do anything to be with You

still, You seem so far away

usually I think it's all well in hand

but tonight I feel confused

I tried to rectify a wrong impression

it seems the messages got confused

I've been carrying inner conflict

it turned to anger when You refused

to let me bring You pleasure

You said that You weren't in the mood

You've guilt-tripped yourself out

I felt rejected by and by

my anger reached new levels

I don't know exactly why

I will respect your wishes

if You say "why don't we take our clothes off

lie down and hug and touch

but not make love"

if you make me understand how You feel

and if You know why You want what You want

of course I'll be with You

in whatever way is best

but don't have your body saying "do"

while your mouth is saying "don't"

when You don't want more red hot pleasure

cause your fire at home is burning low.

Tired But Lovely

You were so tired today

it's rough without sleep

still your presence I needed

our love to restate

this weaning is so hard

I don't want to step back

we've gone so fast forward

maybe now we slow down.

Whatever evolves

I miss You too much

and I appreciate your coming by

even when you're worn out.

But my God, your beauty

and such a sweet smile

I want You forever

and I want You now.

As time went by and May and I continued seeing each other, her husband became more and more uncomfortable with the open marriage arrangement. He was taking advantage of it, but not as much as May was. He wasn't in love with his diversion, he feared she was.

They talked about giving up on the open marriage and going back to normal monogamy. So despite everything she'd told me and everything we had felt and done, she was offering to give me up.

Moon Kiss

I blew You a kiss with the Moon above my shoulder

    as I watched You drive away

we finally let our love come out

    but first my anger was displayed.

You sought it out and brought it up

    You felt it hiding there inside

for I'd been offered as a sacrificial lamb

    one too many times

With a touch Love reassured us

    there was never any doubt

still, You search for vague solutions

    in a Night that offers naught.

Time flows by and in its wake

    we find ourselves adrift

but we have this summer to live and love

    for now, that's all there is.

Not Laughing

You feel the pressure of your work

and things aren't wonderful at home

You've offered, twice, to give me up

an attitude not my own

it's a perspective that I have to face

instead of brood for days

until You bring it out to be resolved

and the next night laid away.

You didn't smile your love at me this week

You didn't smile or laugh at all

but you're getting lots of work done

another crisis point we've survived

and I'm sure that I love You

A love which You return

don't let this drive You crazy

just keep on keeping through.

The Weeping Whiners of Your Life

How dare You lump me in with all your weeper-whiners

I'm the only one in your life, maybe the only one

    in your whole world

Not bitten by the weakness bug.

How dare You get mad at me, and then complain about it

    to your husband.

You're crazy.

<u>You</u> called and offered me your company

    I accepted   -   I didn't beg or plead

or need to take your precious time, especially when you're busy

    and have deadline you can't meet

But don't ever waste a second of my time

    if You don't want to be with me

then fine, it's simple   -   don't.

Your visit last night was worse than your absence

      that was your doing, not mine

And I've never asked You for a fucking cent

      so don't insult, hint, or imply

that that has ever been my game

      that's nothing but a lie

it's common sense

      if You have excess money

and I don't

      that you'll spend more

I always did in the same situation

      that's just the way life goes

It was only when I felt used that I ever resented

      if You feel used

            Be gone.

Gentle Rest

I've known some pain filled nights

    that bestowed in me the certainty

        that Death must be a gentle rest.

And on occasion I did seek to sleep

    or find that gentle rest

        a certain peace

that eternal still of Night that Death must be

As time went by my flirtations with Death grew in boldness

    and as I failed, but came too close

        I began to change my way of thinking

And now that love has thawed my heart

    and now that I sleep every night

I know the certainty of my own desire

    to continue life, and I'll be alright.

Still, I so strongly want You

I seem to grow in needing You

I love to grow in loving You

And I want so much to live Life fully

so much, so much   -   because of You

and because of our love.

Missing You

        I hear a song pounding out a lie on the radio

        with every beat it reminds me

        of what I didn't want to know

        there's a lie pleading in every line

        he says he ain't missing her at all

        but he sings the song with fire

        and You know he needs her love

        and I feel it all tonight

        all the lonely nights to come

You're moving to teach two hours away

and You say it's pull-back time

But it's not just what You said to me

but the strange sound of your voice

when You say we've got to cut it back

Do You mean time, or You mean love?

And I feel it all tonight,

heartaches coming one by one

all the lonely, lonely nights

aching for Your touch

and as I hear that singer lying, pleading

I know just what he wants

I just want to be where You are, happy

not singing damn sad songs.

No, I ain't missing You at all

I spend my time on other things

I don't think about You all the time

and You never cross my dreams.

No, I ain't missing you at all

I spend my time on other things

I don't think about you all the time

and you never cross my dreams.

Pull-Back Time

For nine months now I've tried so hard

    to do everything I can

To give You the respect and love

    that I would think your life demands

And now You say it's pull-back time

    that we knew it had to come

Well You can pull the time away

    but would You pull away in love?

I've seen You, with me, arrive at peace

I've seen You cuddled in my arms

I've seen the warmest smile of all my life

And eyes that shined pure love.

And I've counted as enchanted

      the love filled time we've had together

All that, plus all the love I have

      is why I won't be letting go.

If You Were Available

When I tried to tell You I felt anxious

needing to clear up a false impression

it's because You say it's bad at home

and You might have to take some action

I've said I'd marry You tomorrow

when I know I mean in years

if You were free tomorrow

I'd say let's live together first

You say I'm getting tired of You

but that's not what I mean

this is purely hypothetical

but I had to set it straight

<u>If</u> You ever really left him

I'd want a trial run before the ring.

As these last poems indicates, things between May and I had become more and more strained. She was going to be living at a college about an hour and a half away from Atlanta. She and her husband continued talking about their options. She told me that we had to pull back some. She told me to find a female friend in Atlanta to date, etc. She said it was too much pressure to try to do her job, keep her husband, keep her sanity, and satisfy my desires for her company.

A couple of weeks after telling me that it was pull back time and to find another friend, she came over to my place one day in a very serious mood, explaining that it was make-it or break-it time for her marriage. She and I had fallen deeply in love in a short time. We had talked about a possible future together and marriage. But we had talked about it in the future, more as a fantasy or a dream than an imminent reality. This is a behavior very common among lovers, despite age or situation.

For some reason, being a psychologist, it bothered May greatly that her first marriage had failed and her second one was in jeopardy. It was as though she thought the tools of psychology could prevent fluctuations of the heart or the breakdown of relationships. It was like she thought she had failed as a psychologist because her marriages weren't perfect. What marriages are?

I had used the phrase before, "that I would marry her tomorrow if she was free". As serious as she was on the day of her visit, I told her that if she were to get divorced, I thought we should live together for awhile and then get married. My attempt at honesty and rational thinking was not appreciated by her in the least. Although there was no negativity in my words or heart, and I thought I was telling her what I could realistically offer, that was not how she took my words at all. She took my words as some kind of rejection, while I thought I had just offered to marry her at some rational period after her divorce, if she ever got one. Hell knoweth no furry like a woman scorned, or even one who falsely projects she'd been rejected.

When you first fall in love you have a very natural, wishful tendency to see that person as the fulfillment of your dreams. When I was in California studying with Eve Eaton she told me that falling "in love" was an illusion, an ego-stroke. I wouldn't go that far, I think the feeling of falling in love is one of the most wonderful offered in all of Nature. But I would say that falling in love is a kind of insanity. You tend not to be your normal everyday rational self when you first fall in love. When you first fall in love there is a strong tendency to fall into believing that your lover is who you've been waiting to love, and they see you as you really are, the way you want to be seen. Of course, as time goes by, these illusions begin to fall away and reality begins to dawn. By then you start to see your lover's darker side, their faults and weaknesses. Just as they've seen yours. Although I was still enthusiastically in love with May, we had loved long enough to see each other's darker sides.

She had often told me she was shallow at depths. I had begun to believe her. There were times she showed an appalling lack of understanding of basic human nature. Especially for someone in her chosen profession. This dichotomy had been underscored by a conversation we once had. I'd asked her why she had majored in psychology and she had responded because it was so challenging. She knew I had made nothing but A's in all the psychology courses I had taken (it was my minor), and asked me why I hadn't pursued it more.

I told her it was just too easy, too common sense. A lot of it was stuff I felt any human should intuitively understand.

Her expertise was in educational psychology, which was good because she didn't have patients. I never thought she had a great love for or empathy with her fellow human beings. It was possibly such thoughts that may have prompted my clarification of the "marry you tomorrow" comments. They seemingly doomed our relationship.

We went into the school year with her away during the week, and seeing me on the weekend when she had spare time. She and her husband were working on making it work.

Her reaction to my clarification of the marriage situation, was something I didn't understand. If she got divorced, I thought she would want some time before getting remarried. But she took it as a rejection. The ironic thing, if she had gone off on a weekend and gotten a Mexican divorce, I would have married her the next day.

I was still crazy in love with May, but not stupid. Between her job, her husband, and me, I was coming in third and she had offered to give me up. She wasn't making much time for me so I took her serious when she said find a friend so there would be no pressure on her to try to keep two men happy. My clarification of my marriage comments may have doomed our relationship, but Gabrielle was the hammer that drove the nails in the coffin.

Now this is a whole different subject, Gabrielle and sibling rivalry. My brother Winslow and I are only 13 months apart. We are very close and have a very strong love bond. But from the time of adolescence on, we had a fairly strong case of similar interests and sibling rivalry when it came to the opposite sex.

Over the years we had dated girls that the other one had dated before, not a lot, but it happened. On a camping trip I didn't go on, he had once hit on my ex-love Peggy while we were still together. She rebuked him but it still pissed me off. But he thought one of his ex-girlfriends and I had gotten together immediately after they broke up. He never quite believed me that we hadn't become lovers and had just remained friends.

The latest incident in the long history of sibling rivalry was with my previous love Carol. I brought Carol from Athens to meet Winslow when he was working as a bouncer at an Atlanta niteclub. I wanted him to meet my new lady love. He had been half-drunk and tried playing footsie with her under the table, which she had informed me of the second we left the club. I felt like I still owed him one. That's why I didn't hesitate with Gabrielle.

Winslow's next door neighbor was a reggae fan who loved to go to Jamaica. He returned from a trip there with a beautiful German woman, Gabrielle. She had learned to speak English in her years living in Jamaica so she spoke Jamaican English with a German accent. It was incredibly cute.

To make a long story short the neighbor had gotten her out of some kind of jam by bringing her home. Winslow stole her from the boy next door. I stole her from him.

In my defense May had told me to find a playmate and I was still resentful towards Winslow about Peggy and Carol. Gabrielle started dropping by my place. I told Winslow about it, and in his most confident, almost sneering voice, he said, "If you get a chance, go for it."

Gabrielle was mine in two weeks. Now Gabrielle (she pronounced it Gah-bree-a-lah) knew all about May, and I reported to May that I had found a playmate. In fact, Gabrielle told me that she wanted to be loved like I loved May. It was only later that I understood she wanted me to love her like I loved May. Sometimes I'm just not too quick. Like believing May about getting another female friend.

May was cool with everything on the phone. She told me she didn't care at all as long as my new companion was not a serious rival. She wasn't, my heart was

May's. But I was enjoying a little pay-back on Winslow. Who wasn't thrilled that now I had two girlfriends, one of whom had been his.

May never ceased to amaze me at how honest she had been with both her husband and myself. So I wasn't too surprised when she told me she wanted to meet Gabrielle, just to make sure she wasn't a serious rival. Sometimes I'm just not too quick. I agreed.

So I warned Gabby (Gah-by) and took May to meet Gabrielle at the restaurant/bar where she'd gotten a job as a waitress. Gabrielle waited on us. I introduced everybody, Gabby took our order and walked away. Before she got to the bar May informed me that Gabrielle <u>was a serious threat</u>. I tried to convince May that she wasn't. Sometimes I'm just not too quick.

May told me to give up Gabrielle. I wasn't thrilled and didn't rush to the task, but I did. Then after giving up Gabby, I get a surprise call from May.

The Fall Means Winter Comes Autumn `84

Cold Hard Words on the Phone

When I heard your cold hard words on the phone tonight

      they hit me like a sledgehammer

shattering the mirror of my soul

      I felt and saw that mirror

shattering in shards of glass

      sparkling, reflecting light, and falling

leaving just an empty space

      and pain.

My body goes into a state of shock

      it cools, and cools, and trembling begins

I grow colder and feel hollow

      the shaking more intense.

"We'll be lovers forever"

      I remember saying it

"we'll be lovers forever"

      I remember You saying it

I can still hear it in your soft sweet voice

      hear it said with conviction and strength

and I believed it.

      Must I stop believing?

Expecting You to Call

I've been expecting You to call me up

to apologize for your rude attack upon my sanity

I'm appalled that our relationship carried no more meaning to you

than to be terminated with pure tackiness on the telephone

God knows what bullshit You must have been neurotically projecting

or had You lain in wait for months and months

for your husband's overwhelming magnanimous offer of monogamy

in exchange

for one sacrificial love.

But yet no call

no insincerely voiced apology for the utter rudeness at your home

You gave your lack of depth away

and exposed your like-mother like-daughter cuntness

You hit new lows

and yet, despite the pain

despite this empty hollow deadness here inside

I cannot cease my love for You

my concern about your health, your happiness, your well-being

and I hope that some day

some day not so far away

You come more into touch with your human-ness

somehow work past the isolation

somehow find some inner peace

and learn how to stop, be silent, and still.

Don't Tempt the Barely Saved

You tempt the barely saved too much

my choice adjoining me to the Light

was not an overwhelmingly clear decision

You tempt too much

Never has my pride and dignity

my sanity, my taste, and my humanity

ever been so rudely and tactlessly attacked

without violent or psychological retribution

I sit in anger still amazed

at that total lack of feeling or compassion

so often bought with too much wealth

that makes the little rich bitch act so ruthless

it's a heartlessness so often bought

with the sweat of the lessors

to fill the coffers of the betters.

Even during your tryout as a radical

they saw your game

and read You as You really are

intelligent but unreal

fascinated and perplexed

by the humanity of which You aren't a part

and probably never will be

I ponder back and forth

your words of love

and weigh them against your gain

the goal You must have had all along

monogamy

You got your way

and though I can't forget

these last ten months of love

a love not unflawed

but in my eyes, a love

that could have filled my lifetime

I made mistakes

but none that equal

your neurotic false projections

You threw away strong love

without giving me the opportunity

to sacrifice

something for our love

and the utter lowness to which You sank

to facilitate our parting

has helped me deal with all this hurt and pain

for as totally as I've cherished You these last ten months

I'll stay hurt and angry at You for ten months more.

Tactless

I look at poems of love

I wrote You just a week ago

really just five days

and can't believe the changes that came to be

I look at my mistakes

how You did warn, but wouldn't say

would not pronounce your jealousy

I told You I would give You what You wanted

You should have plainly said

"I'm jealous

don't be with her again."

I would have complied

I would have complied

when school began again this fall

with You two hours away for most of the week

and a husband to satiate

You yourself, two weeks ago

told me to find someone in town

a friend with which to hang around

and when I do just as you've said

You push away so hard, so quick

with such bad taste

the little rich bitch so tactless on the phone

when I was twelve years old

I knew better than that

"it's over" statements don't belong on the telephone

but between two people in the flesh

communicating

You were so tactless, hard, and cruel

I feel my anger, outweighing my love

and so it goes, it's over, at least for now

and from the sound of your voice at times

I can almost believe you've let it die within your heart

You were a gift of the Gracious Goddess

maybe for a week I forgot

to treat You as a sacred gift of the Goddess

manifest within my life

But You don't see things clearly

it's not that you're naive

but in our ten months together I've never understood

what it is about your fellow humans being

that you, so deeply, don't comprehend

but maybe that's why there's no peace within your heart

no peace within your spirit

no peace within your soul

and maybe <u>that's</u> what makes You cold enough

to treat me mean and say the things You did

good God, I loved You with a fervor

that deserved better words than these

your cold rejection

But maybe it's all working out okay

at least You and your husband have a marriage now

and not what You had for a year

a hollow, false charade

and maybe it's good You show me now

that You <u>always have to get your way</u>

that you overreact to situations

You misread or misunderstand

You tell me to grow up

but you don't "get" your fellow man

the things You find perplexing are simply human

there is no great deception here

I found out so long ago

unlike the little rich girls

that in real life

You don't always get your way

and so you've pushed away so hard

and convinced yourself I've done You wrong

and crossed the lines You never drew

you never whispered any warning

well fuck you spoiled brat

fuck you bitch

miss my kisses on your face

miss my gentle hands

miss my healing massage

and the peace of the spirit I bring to you

and miss repeated ecstasy

miss me, miss me

miss me time and time again girl

I hope You cry and ache

in those moments you're alone

You pushed away too hard, too quick

I made one mistake with Gabrielle

but I didn't, as You say, rub her in your face

and even if I had, all You had to do was say "enough

enough"

and it would have been

do you forget you've been sleeping with your husband all this time

all this time

but oh no, oh no, the pride and arrogance

of money, class, and culture

and yet so tactless, so unperceptive, so inhumane

it's a shame and I pity You

I pity the way you've removed yourself from Nature

the way You just don't feel the spirit

the way You just don't see Life's Love

and I feel true pity

because, despite losing me and regaining your marriage

You still seem so lost.

Lost in spirit

Lost in soul.

Method of Your Madness

the method of your madness

bore such surprising meanness

I would never try

to sit, and in one hour, say every hurtful thing

that came to mind

it's not my style

and I would hope I'm too humane

and just too sensitive

to the pain I cause in others

I knew that I had made mistakes

mistakes I was in the process of correcting

but I didn't jump by your time scale

I didn't jump fast enough

or high enough

and so You turned on me

with such mean spite

I hardly knew your face

and your words still echo in my ears

so false, so cold

an attempt to create false distance

"I don't like the things we do, anymore

it's over

it's over

You rubbed her in my face

it's over

I said all my pride would allow

it's over

it's over"

You act so rude

and then ask me for my pictures of You back

and had the gall to say you'd paid for them

just like You had so many hotel rooms

You no longer trust me

You wouldn't listen to the words I spoke

and You spoke words

You didn't mean

to sound just right

while You couldn't come to grips

with your own heart

and so we're over

yet in a way

one of the sweetest loves of my life

by ending

frees me.

Every Time

I thought about it long and hard

it comes out bullshit every time

I try to see things your way.

Let's face it You just turned me out

when You knew You had your husband back

and that's all there is to it.

When did I deny You anything

when did I act rude

or turn You away?

That time You sounded serious

that You might really leave your husband

I said I'd thought about it deeply

and that I didn't want to be married yet

but that I would love to marry You

and that if You were to leave

I would ask You please, live with me

and I promised You monogamy

that's how I would love for it to be

but You couldn't see

I really meant it

Just like I couldn't see

that I shouldn't believe it

when You told me I was free

You didn't mean it.

I should have known better.

Not Your Buddy

My fingernails have grown

so has my beard

I kept my nails so short for You

just like I kept my moustache trimmed

with You in mind

so many aspects of my life

my hopes, my dreams, my secret thoughts

were built around You

and You shattered that foundation

without the slightest hesitation

without the simplest of warnings

You demolished our pretty house of cards

in one foul swoop

and then You say to me, so cavalierly

that I would survive

and I will survive

but I will not be trifled with

I will not have my deepest set emotions

be made fun of

I will not let You

presuming like some god

destroy and end our love

and in a measly three week time

attempt to resurrect our relationship

transformed, for You,

into a so convenient sex-less friendship

You can not trifle with my love

and your rejection will not crush me

and as time goes by, I have no doubt

that someday, your manipulations laid to rest

You will realize that from your own shallowness

it is You who loses.

Gabrielle Draws Beside Me

I'm not crazy in love with her, like I was with You

but I grow crazier every day

and what I have is warm enough

to keep that rock hard wall away

I avoid an inner hurting

and won't admit to those mistakes

that would justify your actions

or make that ugly scene make sense

So I hold on to my anger

because I know I have to face

I was used to reconcile your marriage

I filled your need   -   got pushed away.

Handcuffs

When I was seventeen and wild

      the first time that I got busted

they put the handcuffs on me and laughed

      when I struggled they felt tighter

and now I think of You and me

      and I still try to understand

I always gave You what You asked for

    within a two week span

This time You decided not to ask

    they were simple words to say

too late You explain your bullshit rules

    You simply pushed my love away

So now, You want a eunuch friend

    and You ask me twist around

so You can put your handcuffs on

    for the first time, I turn You down.

Gabrielle

    I made the woman come so hard she cried   -   both times

    I was an artist at my craft

    whose art was well reciprocated

    with enthusiastic and gymnastic ardor

and still, barely one short hour later

I think of You, I miss your face

I ache to reach out and touch You

so many times during every day

so many moments throughout every day

You rule my mind

and lead this muddled heart of mine

once more, astray

Your talk dissects so much

where is the love?

You talk about emotional truth

but all I see is cold calculation

Mixed with a touch of rash decisions

why couldn't things work

I Refuse

I will not be a lap dog boyfriend

    there to fill the empty hour's need

I won't stand as a gelding eunuch

    helpless at the harem gate.

I remember being denied the curtesy

    of using your telephone

I remember being asked to leave

    two or three times, or more

I remember how You talked about me

    to your husband, on the phone

I will not forget your harsh disdain

    how You belittled me at your home

When I expressed heart-felt emotions

    You stooped low enough to say

I could skip a great performance

    that it was over, anyway

You showed so little self-respect

    You showed zero dignity

and You wouldn't admit until the last

    You gave me up for monogamy

Not Alone

I wonder how You think of me?

I wonder how often?

I ponder whether You used me ruthlessly, for long

or did You just grasp at opportunity?

I had intimations of your true inner nature

I had hints of that cold blond Nazi will

but I had never felt its frozen waves

crashing on my heart before

before those last two tacky days

God graced You with so many talents

You were always quick to claim

how did You become socially so graceless?

Your behavior I disdain.

I wonder about these things so often

but as You had steadfastly predicted

I choose to go through my sorrow   -   not alone

for my sanity I treasure

so I experienced my sorrow with a companion

with the woman I had pushed away

in a useless attempt to retain your love

the woman understood me, and forgave

She's a good woman

You know, a woman

a woman

a woman who did things you'd never stoop to do

she cleaned my house

she made my bed

she wore me out all day

or else all night

a woman, whose body, unlike yours

was not too hyper-sensitive

so she could indulge in love

give herself fully to love

relax and incline to love

and make love <u>repeatedly</u>

not this once

or maybe twice on a hot night bullshit

she holds me all night long

and wakes me hungrily in the morning

she's the kind of woman you chose never to become

which is a shame for me

a shame for your re-born husband

just a shame and waste, period.

But as I see these words

there is much truth

but also many lies

I stayed so sick at heart

I wouldn't love

I couldn't love

I couldn't touch for weeks

I held on to what warm security was offered

and was thankful

and waited for the worst to pass

so much of my world

was built so solidly around You

I know your daily schedule

I know so much of everything about You

and although I'm far from lonely

You really shocked me with your cruelty

and my anger at You remains.

Worse Than Me

I gave You power in my world

You know that you've abused it

I know I hurt You when I whored

but your husband had You more than I did

You always hurt me with the truth

You said that You were being honest

so when You told me I was free

if I wasn't, why'd You say it?

You play with power like a child

You hurt when hurting isn't needed

You don't see the damage that You do

You don't clean up the broken pieces

Even if I make You look and touch

I can't make You see or feel it

the river of my love raged at your dam

seeking a way around or through it

I've met my challenge in this lifetime

it was live or die then

I chose the path of Light and Love

but now it seems that love deserts me

You laugh and think that I'm absurd

when I reveal my inner feeling

those are the moments when I hate

a hate of pain and love's denial

You knew the depth of my devotion

how all others paled within your shadow

You struck me like the silent snake

the viper strikes without a rattle

As your cold poison raced into my heart

I watched the world of my heart shatter

You weakly grin, and say I'm fine

that I won't ever be too lonely

I just hope You miss me till it hurts

then I hope it's just beginning

I want You to ache and need my touch

the gentle stroking of my fingers

I want You to die alone each night

thinking of long and lingering kisses

and I want You to feel that hollow emptiness inside

and ache to hold, and see me smiling

and I want You to feel over, and over, and over again

that "empty pit of the stomach - cold hand choking the heart -

I want to die" feeling

and I want You to ache and suffer

even - if possible

if humanly possible - worse than me.

Having Peace

I drove home and marveled at the Moon

Half a golden orb, surrounded

by three full circles of light

the stars were clear and bright

the whole city just reborn

the day before   -   a strong cleansing rain

this city baptized and transformed

and tonight the city's christened

under the stars and Moon's soft light

a gentle breeze is blowing

and I love the magic Night

and, of course, my mind still turns to You

of who else would I think?

It's two weeks since I tried your way

and now I'm more at peace

Like You, I communicated by hurting

and I got the needed space

I could not be your gelding friend

or forgive You overnight

and then your husband calls and asks me, please, to stay away

and I said alright, I said yeah, okay.

Husband Calling

Well for right now we are over

    who know's how long it'll be

before we try again, if ever

    and I thought we'd make it clean

I never meant to hurt You

    or thought things would be this way

Your husband calls up, but doesn't threaten

    but asks nicely that I stay away

There was nothing much that I could say

    except what would do more harm

I listened while he ranted and raved

    and kept repeating the phrase "my wife"

After the call I locked my door and loaded my .357

    I guess weeks ago You had to decide

he obviously needs You more than I do

    when I said no marriage at this point

I was being hypothetical

    I had no premonition that in two weeks time

that all we had would be thrown over.

You can't grasp human nature

    and You think I'm a whore

I made you reigning queen of my heart

    I guess You wanted more.

Your Husband Asks Me to Stay Away

        I heard his anger on the phone

        I heard the sound of desperation

        He may not love You more than me

        But I don't doubt he needs You deeper

He probably Loves You more than me

Everybody says I'm just a tom-cat

But I held back so many things

Things I could have said, but didn't tell him

I didn't tell him You seduced me

I didn't mention hotel rooms

or who helped with my rent money

I didn't say a thousand things

that could only hurt your marriage

I didn't say a fucking thing

about how he got my unlisted number

I didn't say You called me first

or mention by-gone propositions

I didn't say a fucking thing

I just let him scream and holler

I just let him scream and holler

I didn't use my opportunity

to wreak real havoc on your marriage.

Supposed To Do

I know what I'm supposed to do

      is just let it all go

You and your husband reunited

      our love of a year is no more

You never would tell the whole truth

      but You weren't really ever a liar

until the end when the truth came out

      You trashed our love to rebuild your marriage.

All Love's Must End

All loves must end somehow

        except maybe

                the One Love

but I didn't like your break-up style or cruelty

        I found your theatrics unnecessary

            and your method sadistic

that's just how I feel

        yet I am grateful for the beauty of what we had

            grateful for Life and an unknown future.

The Bitter Risk of Sweet Adultery

As I live my daily life

this day to day life without You in it

I kick myself inside

to think that I could be so greedy

All my needs fulfilled

all the love that I could handle

still I had to grab for more

You just blamed it on my lifestyle

If I'd had a thought, or clue, or hint

that You might reject me so completely

I might have done things differently

I'd have given You no reasons

But You did exactly what You did

and it may have saved your marriage

so now, I'm all alone, outside

the bitter risk of sweet adultery.

Mimosa Blooms in the Summertime

The Mimosa blooms in the Summertime

hues of purple, pink, and peach

a soft and sensual flower blossoms

till Summer's end, from early Spring

I tried to catch that endless Summer

we shared a love spun from a dream

But You halted love at Autumn's coming

before the leaves fell from the trees

With the fallen seed is the promised coming

of the blossoms in the Spring

and though the future now remains unknown

I'll survive dark Winter's pain.

Mimosa Untouched by Winter's Storms

The Mimosa seeds hang in the trees still

untouched by Winter's furious storms

It seems an endless Indian Summer

It's almost December, yet the air grows warm

This time last year the dance was courtship

in shadows, shades, in hints, and looks

we came so far, so fast, so deeply

what we felt in heart we shared in soul

it's left me shocked, surprised, bewildered

at one year's rise, and one year's fall

So now I dance and twirl in Shadows

by myself and all alone

my love we danced so well together

we danced so well the Dance of Love.

After the Fall Winter `84, and 1985

To recap the obvious, May ditched me on the phone and I went back to Gabrielle and she took me back. Which was nice after I dumped her for May. And then May starts calling up wanting to be friends and her husband starts calling to ask me to leave her alone. So I leave her alone and Gabrielle and I were doing pretty well. It wasn't the kind of love I had for May but we were good lover/friends and that was enough for both of us. I still thought about May some, but I was moving on.

There was one slight problem. It turned out was Gabrielle was an international smuggler by profession. Life is always full of surprises. She began in her profession smuggling Germans out of Communist East Germany. Certainly a patriotic beginning. But when the commies wised up to her and she could no longer work that trade, she began carrying packages across borders for money.

Actually it seemed pretty glamorous, dating an international smuggler, and since I wasn't involved in her business, I didn't worry about it that much. She had told me she was pretty much just doing the occasional run of hash oil and exotic herb from Jamaica.

On Christmas Eve I got a call from jail. Gabrielle didn't make it through the airport.

Deportee

They're playing "Smuggler's Blues" on the radio

and I love to sing the blues

They say you just can't stop it

money too good to refuse

and Gabrielle's out of jail

just call her deportee

Eastern flew her back to Jamaica

the drug paradise at sea

And me, I got her friend Andrea out

she'd been in for just two months

but she sure don't want to go back

didn't like the food too much

and I hear it in my heart and soul

those dear old smuggler's blues

that the money's too damn good and fast

too damn good to be refused

> but me, I know it's bullshit
>
> just like those who've done hard time
>
> the money made is seldom saved
>
> what's mostly left is sad, wrecked lives.

Gabrielle got busted in the Atlanta airport on Christmas Eve. They deported her a couple of weeks later. I got regular cards from her, until they stopped after her last one from Bangkok. Maybe she just quit writing. I eventually asked everyone who knew her, all her letters and cards stopped at the same time. All I could do was pray she was alright. I didn't think much about her not writing at first, but now I tend to think she may be dead or in jail. I hope she just gave up on her American friends since she couldn't come back. Because of her lifestyle and profession, its not easy to be optimistic. She might have made some mistakes but she was a sweet soul and God bless her.

It was only natural that I would think of May as time went by, just as I did Gabrielle, and write poems as I reflected.

Spring Rain

The Spring rain is falling gently outside

I go to my porch to smoke and think

the honeysuckles are beginning to flower

at night the fireflies are beginning to mate

This time last year our love was endless

wrapped in newness   -   tied with mystery

we touched discovering the richness of each other

in emotional, mental, and sensual ways

my heart was given and so was yours

our only problem your husband at home

and You were determined not to leave him

yet make our relationship last and grow

How naive it seems in retrospect

that with love so strong we still believed

that no collision lay before us

no foreshadowing I'd be left to bleed

and so I wonder late at night

deep in this emptiness inside

if I could have things as they once were

with the risk of ending in that same style

Would I even want to try

No, I don't think I'd want to try.

Like We Were Sixteen

This time last year it was hotel rooms

    and You usually paid the bill

I was ship-wrecked at my parents

    You were a marriage-escapee

Now that you're back to your marriage

    and your, for me, too normal life

in your strange, so very strange marriage

    do You think of me at night?

Do You think of the pleasure You gave me

    when we went parking like we were sixteen

or do You think of the pleasure I gave You

    You were always too easy for me.

In my heart I still can't get past You

    don't <u>believe</u> that you'll stay away

but still, I don't want to get married

    or go through life

        with my heart

            wrapped in chains.

June Night

        The June night is filled with fireflies

        the stars twinkling way up above

        the Mimosa tree's in full blossom

        pink flowers shimmering under the Moon

        The night air is warm and breezy

        the days are long and hot

I lost a love that hurt deeply

nine months later   -   I still feel that loss.

I'm alone a lot, but not lonely

I'm not unhappy, I'm sure not depressed

but nine months ago I was fully in love

now normal life seems so dull and drab

now that passion's fires have cooled

and now I once more stand alone

somehow this life that's lived while not in love

seems something less than whole.

Violent Passages

The violent passages of my gentle life

    arise within my mind

the memories of kind and loving times

    are too easily pushed aside

But when I think upon the love that is, or was

      or is now in abeyance

I think more upon the smiles and little tendernesses

      than of the emotional violence

which marked our ending

      and try as I have for many months

I cannot make it all make sense

      I had and lost so much

without intention

      and with such a harmless attitude

and with such strong love for You

      we had and made bad choices

bad choices

      we had and made bad choices

            and so much was thrown away.

Chance Encounter

A chance encounter

at the grocery store

I finally get to see You

it seems like years have passed

You looked tired and older

You looked unhappy

You always used to smile at me

We shared such joy in our relationship

I put my hands behind my back

so You wouldn't see them shaking

within a few short seconds

You dropped what You were holding

and You tried hard to not look nervous

but we were both pretending.

You Looked So Different

They're watching for tornadoes outside

and it looks just like my soul

ever since You killed our love

I just haven't got a hold

and I feel my grip is slipping

as outside the thunder calls

I'm a child, so much, of Nature

yet for a year You caught my soul.

And I wonder what You feel for me

do You keep our love alive

you've been silent for what seems so long

did You let our true love die?

and what about the future

somehow I still see mine as bright

I'm a writer and a do-er

and a friend of Dark and Light.

But You, You seemed so different

when by accident we met

your eyes were dark

your spirit tired

You seemed in need of rest.

The eyes I saw were not the eyes

that once sparkled into mine

the face I saw was not the face

that smiled love into mine

up close, in love, you're beautiful

a beauty awe inspiring

but when I finally saw your husband and You

instead of envy

I felt sorrow.

www.ingramcontent.com/pod-product-compliance
Lightning Source LLC
Chambersburg PA
CBHW080516090426
42734CB00015B/3071